FOR THEIR SALVATION

VOLUME 2

For Their Salvation
Copyright © 2023 by Kendryana Scharschmidt
All rights reserved.

No part of this book may be reproduced or used in any manner without the prior written permission of the copyright owner, except for the use of brief quotations in a book review.
Disclaimer
Scripture quotation marked ESV are taken from the ESV® Bible (The Holy Bible English Standard Version®).
Copyright © 2001 by Crossway, publishing ministry of Good News Publishers. Used by permission. All rights reserved.
Scripture quotations marked NLT are taken from the Holy Bible, New Living Translation. © 1996, 2004, 2007, 2013 by Tyndale House Foundation. Used by permission of Tyndale House Publishers Inc., Carol Stream, Illinois 60188. All rights reserved.
Scripture quotations marked KJV are taken from the King James Bible Version of the Bible.

License Notes This book and eBook is licensed for your personal enjoyment only. This book and eBook may not be re-sold or given away to other people. If you would like to share this book with another person, please purchase an additional copy for each PERSON, you share it with. Thank you for respecting the hard work of this author. No part of this publication may be reproduced, distributed, or transmitted in any form or by any means, including photocopying, recording, or other electronic or mechanical methods, without the prior written permission of the publisher, except in the case of brief quotations embodied in critical reviews and certain other non-commercial uses permitted by copyright law.

Cover Design by Kendryana Scharschmidt
Publisher's Name Kendryana Scharschmidt

Table of Contents

Introduction

For Their Salvation

My Dream

Chapter 1-
The Refiners Fire

Chapter 3
A Fresh Start

Chapter 2
Separated And Surrendered

Chapter 4
The Journey Back Home

Chapter 5
Desperation The Journey Back To GOD

Chapter 6
Move Forward

INTRODUCTION

FOR THEIR SALVATION

This is a testimony about a marriage that had to go through the refiner's fire, to be made pure as gold. In the book of Job, Job was referred by GOD.

Now I don't know about you, but I been referred for jobs, scholarships, even by my clients to their friends and family. But being referred by GOD Himself to the devil, to be tested and tried isn't something I would volunteer for.

I'm remembering In Luke chapter 22 verse 31, when JESUS spoke to Simon and said Satan has desired to have you, that he may sift you as wheat.

As I was reading, I was waiting for JESUS to respond in a way that would stand up for Simon. Maybe something like, "But I told him no."

Yet, He didn't respond that way. His response was anything other than what "Man" would presume "THE SAVIOR OF THE WORLD" would give. A response to keep us safe from the evil one.

    NO, JESUS'S reply was one that could only come from heaven. One that was higher than our ways, or our understanding. He replied, "But I have prayed for thee, that thy faith would fail not: and when thou art converted, strengthen thy brethren.
(Some versions translate: "And when you have come through the time of testing, turn to your companions and give them a fresh start," meaning- help them too.

FOR THEIR SALVATION

In this testimony, of the trying of my marriage, and the trying of my faith. I have come to understand that everybody wants a "Kingdom Marriage," but nobody wants to be asked for. Nobody wants to be recommended for the trying and testing of their faith. To undergo being purified, and to come out pure as gold.

I now see it as a spiritual (boot camp.) Training, to earn a badge in marriage. Once you've come out of the fire and the testing, you are now then called to go and help your brethren. Others who are struggling in their marriage. You are then called to now show them the way as well.

We fight the good fight not only for ourselves, but for others around us, and the generations to come.

Kendryana Scharschmidt

FOR THEIR SALVATION

VOLUME II

Hey Papa,

Friday September 3rd
11:40am

    I haven't written in a long time. There's so much I want to get out. First, I'm noticing the spiritual and physical separation that you're doing between Nick and me. I keep hearing you say to separate from him and to stop talking to him. LORD, at first, I didn't understand. I was frustrated, angry, lost, confused, and misplaced. I love my husband; I couldn't understand why you would make us separate like that.

    I'm not sleeping in the bed, were not making love, and we're not speaking like that.

    My mind keeps going back to when you first came to me about loving him too much, to the point, to where we made each other our gods. You said we idolized each other. We would do anything for each other, but then I thought that's how marriage is supposed to be. Right? And you had to then show me. NO!! Thats how the world says marriage is supposed to be, but who made marriage in the first place, you asked.

    You did LORD, I replied. And then you begin to press on my heart to ask you how marriage is supposed to be.

    In Ecclesiastes chapter four you referred to a "Godly Marriage," as a three-strand cord, that is not easily broken. LORD, now I understand. (Marriage) should include you. Your supposed to be in the center, the main focus. While my husband and I are standing side by side. Like an Isosceles triangle, with only two of its sides being equal.

Lord, I see you moving me out of the way of his life. Just like you're doing in mine. You're tearing us down, breaking us down, and removing all our idols. Forcing us to be broken and brought so low that we are forced to turn to You, and seek your face.

My Dream

(I had a dream that you had separated Nick and I. We were on a train heading north when this great big old man stopped the train, and I knew it was you. And we were lamps, I was turned on, but Nick was grey and broken. His light was not working. You took me off the train, but you left Nick on, laying in the corner. You then let the train go. You carried me away, and I was so mad at you. I was so angry and frustrated, and I kept asking you why he couldn't come to. Why was he not getting off the train too Lord. You wouldn't answer me. You placed me in this big, dark room. As I sat in the corner of that big empty room with tears in my eyes feeling alone and confused. I watched as my sisters stared in pity and sadness for me from the other side of the doorway. When I woke up, I didn't understand, but I see now you're working on us separately. Nick is not ready yet. He hasn't been fully broken yet. Our marriage doesn't look like crap yet, so he's still holding on. He hasn't surrendered yet.

Lord, we just had an anniversary, and it was the saddest anniversary we have ever had. But I trust you Lord, better days are coming. Once you're done tearing our marriage down and building us a new one, I know our bond is going to be so beautiful. However, first I must go through some things, so that my pain may be written on the pages of this book, so that my husband and I can help other marriages struggling to get their title as a Kingdom Marriage.

CHAPTER 1

THE REFINERS FIRE

"But who may abide the day of his coming? and who shall stand when he appeareth? for he is like a refiner's fire, and like fullers' soap."

Malachi 3:2 KJV

FOR THEIR SALVATION

In this spiritual box of a room, I feel so alone LORD. I know I'm on the potter's wheel, I know I'm being made whole. Cleansed of all my iniquity and purified of all my sin. But papa this hurts. I feel like no one gets me, and the people that do understand what it's like to walk with you, I understand some revelations can't be shared yet. Some testimonies aren't testimonies until you come out with the victory.

My husband thinks I'm crazy. I read the book of Psalms, and it's funny how you don't understand a scripture's meaning until your actually going through what the writer is experiencing. David spoke in psalm 38 about his sin, his separation from his family and your hand against him. Lord, I know we need these times in our life of isolation, refinement, and discipline by your hand. It shapes and molds us into the men and woman you ordained for us to become.

I've been fasting like never before with you. I feel your presence so strong leading me closer to you, but away from Nick. I'm so lost, you've been teaching me how to pray for my husband, and how to war on his behalf. How to stand in the gap for him while he's still in the dark and living in sin. You've also been showing me myself. My sin, and where I fall short as a wife. I've been learning how to uplift, and encourage my husband, instead of putting him down. Yet, you're pulling at my heart to come out from amongst him. To come forward as a righteous daughter of the KING, with no one else dimming my light. I feel called and set apart.

The beginning of last year, you called me to a forty-day water fast. I thought either my life was over, or I was going to ask you to take me right then and there. There was no way I was going to disobey you, but I couldn't see past the first day either. Going into the journey I remember thinking; I could never do anything like this I'm not JESUS. But you brought me out. OH LORD, how faithful are you. I'm still alive, and I made it through. It was one of the hardest things I EVER had to do, but it was the MOST AMAZING thing I EVER experienced. During the fast Nick sat down with me down one day and asked me if, when I was done fasting, could he take me out to dinner for my birthday.

  Since the fast went through my birthday month I was unable to eat food and celebrate how everyone else thought I would. I said I didn't know when it would be over. I didn't want to alarm anyone or speak about the fast you had me doing. I know many would be worried especially my mother who called just to see how much weight I had lost. To see if I was trying to self-sabotage myself. I really wasn't trying to think about food, but I will never forget the day of the morning my fast was over. With barely enough energy, I sat in my prayer closet, where we had met over a million times that past couple of months, and I wept silently. Truly feeling nothing in my body, no desire for anything. Not sex, nor tv, nor people, not even Nick, only you LORD. As I wanted to share my first meal with you, being the trail mix I had been eyeing the last couple of days, I couldn't believe it was finally over. You truly carried me and had so much

FOR THEIR SALVATION

mercy. It was all you. The trail mix tasted like bird food. Nothing tasted the same anymore. The blind folds of deception had been taken off of my eyes. I saw everything for what it really was. Television wasn't the same anymore. Music that didn't glorify you made my soul cringe. I had been with the Holy One of Israel truly, for forty days nothing was better than that. Out of that fast you broke many spiritual strongholds, and demonic oppressions off my life. You also opened the door for me to get accepted and to start Cosmetology School, in the spring.

    I also noticed that during the fast many desires were leaving from my heart. I looked at life totally different. All I wanted was you. It was like I died. And I was someone else, Someone new. I didn't want the old things anymore. I didn't even care about my marriage, whatever you wanted to do with it, and me GOD I was yours to have.

    Many ideas were pouring into my head. Spiritual gifts and talents were submerging from the depths of my soul, I was in awe at your presence LORD. OH MY! What an experience. You had changed my mindset and how I felt about everything.

    A particular day during the fast I distinctly remember I was in the living room at night folding clothes, and my husband came in there to sit with me. Since I wasn't eating, I realized I had ample amount of time to stay busy. I spent the days reading my bible and getting my house in order, physically and spiritually. He looked at me as I continued to fold clothes, and he asked me if I was ok. I replied, yes.

FOR THEIR SALVATION

He then began to spill his heart. He asked me what was wrong with me I hadn't been talking, I don't even make eye contact with him and I'm not eating. He said He realizes he hasn't been a good husband and he's sorry. I listened as he talked, I realized Father, that you had used this fast to heal me. So, when he was finished speaking, I don't think I responded the way he thought I would. I said Nick, I'm happy. I've been spending time with GOD. I don't have to worry about what's on your phone. I don't have to beg you to spend time with me or nag you to take me on a date. I don't have to worry about what you're doing, or what you're not doing. When you come home late from being with your friends, I don't have to be mad about you for coming home past the time I asked you not to, or even being upset because you haven't checked in. The truth is I don't care anymore. I don't care. And when I said that I felt free, because the truth was, I was free. JESUS had set me free from all my worries and cares, he took my burdens and gave me His. And His yoke was easy, and His burden was light. I used to not be able to sleep when my husband was out late with his friends or at a show. I was afraid to be home without him. Or even to sleep alone. Now I prayed for him, rolled over, and went to bed. I knew I was safe in my Father's arms. I was blossoming as a flower; he knew it and so did I.

After I finished the fast, I felt light as a feather. I heard the voice of the HOLY SPIRIT say, now you're walking heavy in the spirit. I cried because I had never felt so close to you

FOR THEIR SALVATION

JESUS in my life, your presence was so strong, chills ran up and down my body and through my face. I knew I was glowing spiritually. After that conversation I saw clearly, we were unequally yoked. I was still praying for him every morning and asking you to heal and deliver him every night. But it wasn't until a day in prayer when I heard you tell me to leave Nick, that this separation became real. You told me to tell him I wanted a divorce. It was very disturbing to say the least but deep down I felt like this relationship was burdening my cross, like it was making it heavy to carry me and him. But having to get a divorce that was the ultimate pain come true. What! No Papa please don't make me do this. I mean yes, I felt like it was dying, but actually letting go like that was on a whole other level I didn't think it would come to.

Some days went by, and I heard you say to tell him now. Immediately heat fumes went through my pores as sweat dripped down my top lip. Now GOD? I was nervous, not knowing what to say, I headed for my prayer closet, seeking courage. I asked him if we could talk, he agreed. Waiting on the leading of the Holy Spirit, I started out by telling him we both wanted different things. He proceeded to tell me not to tell him what he wanted. This was so hard to do. I wanted my marriage. Here I am fighting for something, and God you're telling me in order to save it, I must to let it go. I didn't understand. The pain was deeper than tears, I couldn't even cry. My lack of empathy made it look as if it pleased me to watch my husband break in pieces as I asked

FOR THEIR SALVATION

him for a divorce. He cried and asked me why. I said this is what GOD is telling me to do. He got angry and said, GOD wouldn't tell you to do that. I defensively replied yes, He would. He immediately responded, that wasn't GOD, that aint' GOD. Unaware I stepped away from him waiting on the clouds to open and GOD to come and strike him for speaking against His will. I was silent, not knowing what to say to plead my case. I put my head down in silence in prayer. Waiting for the Holy Spirit to tell me what to say if anything could be said after that. I felt like I was on one of those movies where the girl has to tell the boy she can't see him again because her Father said so. Nick stood in silence for a minute trying to hold back tears, then replied, if that's what you want, then ok. Apart of me was angry. Nick didn't fight for me, and GOD was taking away from me the thing I loved, and was fighting for, my marriage, and my husband. Yet, the other part of my being, was relieved. There was this peace I had in me, like I knew this needed to be done. I felt like a caged bird who was limited in how I served GOD because I was handcuffed to someone going the opposite direction. Can two walk together unless the agree? I understood in that moment why we had to be separated. I loved him so much; I loved what we had so much, but I couldn't love anything so much that I was willing to follow it straight to hell. The bible speaks of the man being the head, and that the woman is to submit to following him. The man is supposed to be leading the household, and if he's not following GOD, where are you all going?

CHAPTER 2

SEPARATED AND SURRENDERED

The days past and we were not speaking. This time he had rage in his heart for me. I was about to start cosmetology school and I asked you LORD, how was I going to get there, and who would watch the kids, seeing as how I was a homeschool-stay at home mom, with no car.

After praying about my concerns, you said my sister would take my place where I had left off. I had just designed us a brand new homeschool space in our home. So, leaving the children was bittersweet. You also said to ask Nick to take me school.
Whoa, bomb drop. I couldn't believe you would put me in that position to break his heart and then ask him to help me. I didn't want to ask. I would have rather taken an uber.

I didn't even know how to present the matter to him. I had not been sharing with anybody the wonderful things you had been doing in my life since the fast. I was led by you to start my own clothing line, open my own spa in my house, and so many other ministries. The next day I just flat out told him I enrolled into school, and I start in a week. I asked if he could take me in the morning and pick me up. Confused to how all of this happened so quickly, he motionlessly said yes.

The morning of my first day of school, riding with him was uncomfortable and heartbreaking at the same time. The car was silent as I reminded myself that you said not to talk to him. If I'm being honest something was starting to happen in my life. The more I separated myself from him, the more I saw GOD move and work on my behalf. Favor, doors, and opportunities opened for me almost immediately. Revelation became a normal thing in my life, and the light of GOD was all over me.

One day I was in class and one of my teachers stopped me. She began to say how it was a delight to have me as one of her students, and how the place had brightened up since I been there. She spoke about how my fruit was so pure it was beautiful. I pondered on this for months, seeing is how I was a new christian, I have never heard anyone speaking about fruit in that way. I have fruit? I thought to myself. And what did she see in me that I couldn't see in myself. Yes, I loved GOD, I talked about Him all the time. He was my only friend. Being secluded in the house with toddlers and an eight-year- old and no car will do that to you. I even found myself praying with other students. I was speaking life where there was no hope in lives, but it was all You Father.

I was being used greatly every day at my school. I knew it was Him, because all I wanted to do was help. My heart was saddened. I had compassion on the crowd. So many broken hearts, so many lost sheep. It was like you gave me your heart Lord, so that I could experience what JESUS felt when he saw the crowd. Compassion for GOD's people, the lost. The ones who needed a healer. And the best part was I knew Him. I loved Him, I actually had a personal relationship with Him. It was like how people boast about knowing famous people, and how they know them on a personal level. Only I was in a place of humbleness because the Spirit of GOD was upon me. My flesh had been crucified; I saw no purpose for boasting. These people needed a doctor, not an autograph and I was determined to tell them about the best one there was. I mean isn't that what a broken heart needs.

   I knew the only reason I was able to tell them about Him, was because He fixed mines. Deep down I was still waiting on my promise to come to pass. My own life was broken. I was waiting on a miracle while I was watching GOD transform the lives I was speaking into. I didn't understand, how you can have so much hope and faith for others, that GOD would restore, and transform their lives, while yours is in the process of demolition. The only logical answer was you GOD. All those nights I spent crying and weeping, in your arms. Thinking about my husband's betrayal, baby Nicholas, my sin, and just the pain of walking alone. I didn't know you were getting ready to turn my mourning into laughter. I felt like JESUS, after His wilderness experience. My ministry had taken off.

   The LORD began using me mightily, in such an impactful way. My heart was tender, and I knew it. When I saw things that displeased the LORD, things that I wouldn't normally budge to, I noticed my heart would hurt in an unexplainable way. Saddened by the fallen ways of man, GOD allowed me to feel what He felt in certain situations. My life was His, and I was His servant sent out to help the masses. Whatever He told me to do, I desired and yearned to do it, no matter how hard. Sometimes I would hear the LORD tell me to go minister to a random person in the store. From fear of what people, or my husband would think, I would hesitate, rather than to do what GOD said to do. And when I disobeyed, I was crushed. Paralyzed in sin, and unable to move. I didn't like that feeling so I tried my very best to obey every command, even if it meant embarrassment, or shame.

   Until one day.
The ultimate test came. I was in my prayer closet, when I noticed this particular day felt different. The sun had just rose and I was spending time with you Lord, when I heard you say, "Arise and go. I didn't understand where you wanted me to go. "Where LORD?" I asked, where do you want me to go. Apart of me wanted confirmation, and another part wanted to act like I didn't hear you.

   I began praying and praying, when you sent me to the book of Isaiah chapter 52 verses 1-5. Basically, telling me to get up and come fourth, that you were calling me out of that place I had been. Somehow, that day, understanding didn't come quickly. It still didn't sit well me, so I asked again. You sent me to 2 Corinthians 6:17 "Therefore, come out from among unbelievers, and separate yourselves from them, says the LORD. Don't touch their filthy things and I will welcome you." NLT

 Then my heart dropped, I mean, how clearer can you be. I didn't know where to begin or what to say.
Go? Leave? Where? Why?
I had so many questions and so much frustration. Why do I

have to leave my home. I'm serving you; I'm trying to do right.

Questions raced through my mind. How am I going to tell my husband GOD wants me to leave? What am I going to tell the kids? I had so many questions, and not many answers. I knew there was a since of urgency behind this message and I was at the point in my life where I was tired of waiting on my husband to want GOD that I wasn't about to miss JESUS for his stubbornness. So, I began to quickly pack my things. I felt the hand of the LORD heavy upon me with this word. It wasn't a game.

It had been three years since the LORD came to me and said my husband would cheat on me. I had been fighting for "HIS" salvation, my peace of mind, and our marriage. I stopped and stared while he laid in the bed sleeping not knowing that he was about to be awoken to his whole life being ripped away. With sadness and tears in my eyes, I ran a course of scenes across my life from the first day GOD, came to my family. I was tired. My hand war beaten and my mind overwhelmed. I was ready to let my "Father" fight for me.

I woke Nick up and told him I was leaving. Unfortunately, there was no sad music playing as I walked out the door and him crying behind me. No, it was actually weird. You see I didn't have a car, so I needed him to take me where I was going. Lord, I had heard you repeat my mom's house twice. Which was humiliating because she had one spare guest bedroom downstairs, and she didn't know what was going on in my home. I didn't want to go there. I wanted to stay in my own home, but I humbled myself. I asked my husband to take me there. In disbelief and confusion crumpled on his face, he watched me gather only what was really important, and what the kids really needed and carry it to the car. He asked me why; I told him; this is what I feel like I'm supposed to do. He left it at that.

It always made me furious how my husband was never the type to fight over an issue, that he would let things just be as they were; unanswered and unfinished. However, that day, I was thankful. I didn't have an answer. What was happening was news to me too. Since I have been walking with you LORD, I've learned so many things. One being that you'll call your children to take some faith-based leaps and tell us to do some strange things that the human mind can't process in our understanding to be logical. But when I learned to trust you, I began to see your way was right no matter what it looked like.

When we arrived at my mother's house, I was sad, I broke down crying. My mother was out of town on a work trip, so I was spared of the anxiety of telling her what was going on right away. I was met at the doors by my two sisters. They welcomed me in with the same identical, crumpled look my husband had just minutes before dropping me off. As he sped off, I knew what this was. It was like being in a familiar place again. The dream I had had last year was slowly coming back to me. It was like it was coming to life right before my eyes. I went into my mom's small little bedroom and sat on the bed. As my sisters took the kids upstairs so that I could be alone, I let out the most dreadful sobbing one had ever released. I was angry with GOD. All the fasting, all the praying, all the waring, and I end up here. I yelled at Him.

You promised me a marriage that honored you. You said my husband would be saved, just like you saved me. Now we're separated. Thanks, now he can go be free, cheat on me, and do whatever he pleases. It was like I was being punished and I was trying to help. I was listening to GOD's every word, and my heart started to grow cold and bitter. Still no baby Nicholas, and Nick is still lost. Is this all a game, is this all one big joke.

The silence in the atmosphere, made me remorseful for the things I had just spoken to a faithful, loving GOD. Chills ran across my arms as my soul filled with your presence LORD. The Holy Spirit came and yoked me up out of the pit I was digging with the shovel that the devil seconds before had handed me. This is necessary He said to me. His presence was so strong. Then He gave me the understanding of a spiritual break, that now it was time for me to work on me. GOD was giving me rest and I couldn't even appreciate it. No longer was I in Egypt, yet I still found reason to complain.

When I looked at my situation like that, the trails of tears on my face dried, leaving white tracks. I was now alone with GOD on a whole new level. It was just uncomfortable. What will I tell everyone? What will I tell my mom? How will I explain to the kids were going to be living at Mimi's house for a while, and that you won't see daddy come home from work at night. He won't say prayers and kiss you goodnight. How am I going to get to school? Wow there was so much to figure out, so much to think about. As I looked around the room, I tried adjusting my mind that this would be my knew home now. Well at least until GOD told me I could go back home. all that crying and thinking made me hungry and plus I was ready to get settled in, all the details had to wait.

    That night as I laid across my mom's old oak bed starring at my phone in frustration. He didn't call, text, or come back. I was so furious with him. Why was he ok with the us being separated. Why didn't he just surrender and ask GOD to fix us. He made me feel like I wasn't worth fighting for.

    Quietness filled the room, when my eyes landed on my youngest daughter peeking at me through the covers. Not wanting to wake the other children, I softly asked her why she wasn't sleeping. She whispered she was sad because daddy was alone. She flopped over and my heart froze. All I could think about was how I was fighting on the front line, for us, while he was blinded. I never thought how he must have felt. I'm sure he assumed I wanted to leave him, and get away from his lack of spiritual improvement, despite the several attempts I made to sit down and tried to explain to him where I stood and what was going on in my world. But I knew he couldn't understand. The Lord asked me many times why I was trying to explain spiritual things to a carnal person. I prayed hard for Nick that night. I wanted GOD to comfort him, and make it known that I wasn't trying to hurt him. I was trying to save us. The last thing I wanted to do was hurt my husband, but if this is what it took to save him, his life, and our family, then this is what I had to do. He needed a savior and I had to move out the way because I wasn't Him. I tried, believe me I did, but just like Cinderella's sisters, the shoe didn't fit. I did my part now it was time for me to get out of the way, and let GOD do His.

"JESUS saith unto him, I am the way, the truth, and the life: no man cometh unto the Father, but by me."

John 14:6 KJV

CHAPTER 3

A FRESH START

The Holy City of Israel

Isaiah 52.
Awake, Awake, Kendryana, put on your strength
Put on thy beautiful garments
(The Amor of GOD)
For now therefore shall no more come into thee
the uncirmcised and the unclean.
Remove yourself from the dead places
and get up
Remove thyself from slumbering
Arise and sit down at the feet of JESUS
Release yourself from the things holding you
back, and down, O bound Kendryana.

For thus saith the LORD GOD, Ye have sold
yourselves for nought amd ye shall be redeemed
without money. For thus saith thus saith the
LORD GOD
My people went down aforetime into Egypt to
sojourn there; and the Assyrian oppressed them
without cause

Sunday Febuary
13th

LORD, I did it. I left him. I left my husband yesterday. I left Nick. My heart is confused. Last night I cried. I had a vision of Nick in a dark cave, and I was sitting there with him. With all my bags packed, holding them. Waiting with him, for JESUS to come and get him. And I finally saw myself walking out of the cave with all my bags. Once out, I saw light, it was green pastures, but he was still in the cave stuck calling my name. But I knew I had to move forward, because the only way he could be saved is if he called upon the name of JESUS.

See now I understand I was his god and he was mine. So we kept each other going in a cycle of trying to always rescue each other. But no human can save us (ONLY GOD). The One True Living GOD. If you rely on a human to save you; one, you have made an idol out of them. Two, humans have limits they can only do so much until both of you are stuck in the same cave together.

Nick was my savior, he rescued me from my mom's house. He rescued me from being a single mother. He rescued me from pain, depression, and loneliness... Or so I thought.

GOD did all those things because I put Nick's face on GOD'S work, I made an idol out of my husband. A little ole man, that's just another creation like me. GOD wants me to love him, not idolize him. GOD is going to give us both revelation on the proper way to love and appreciate each other.

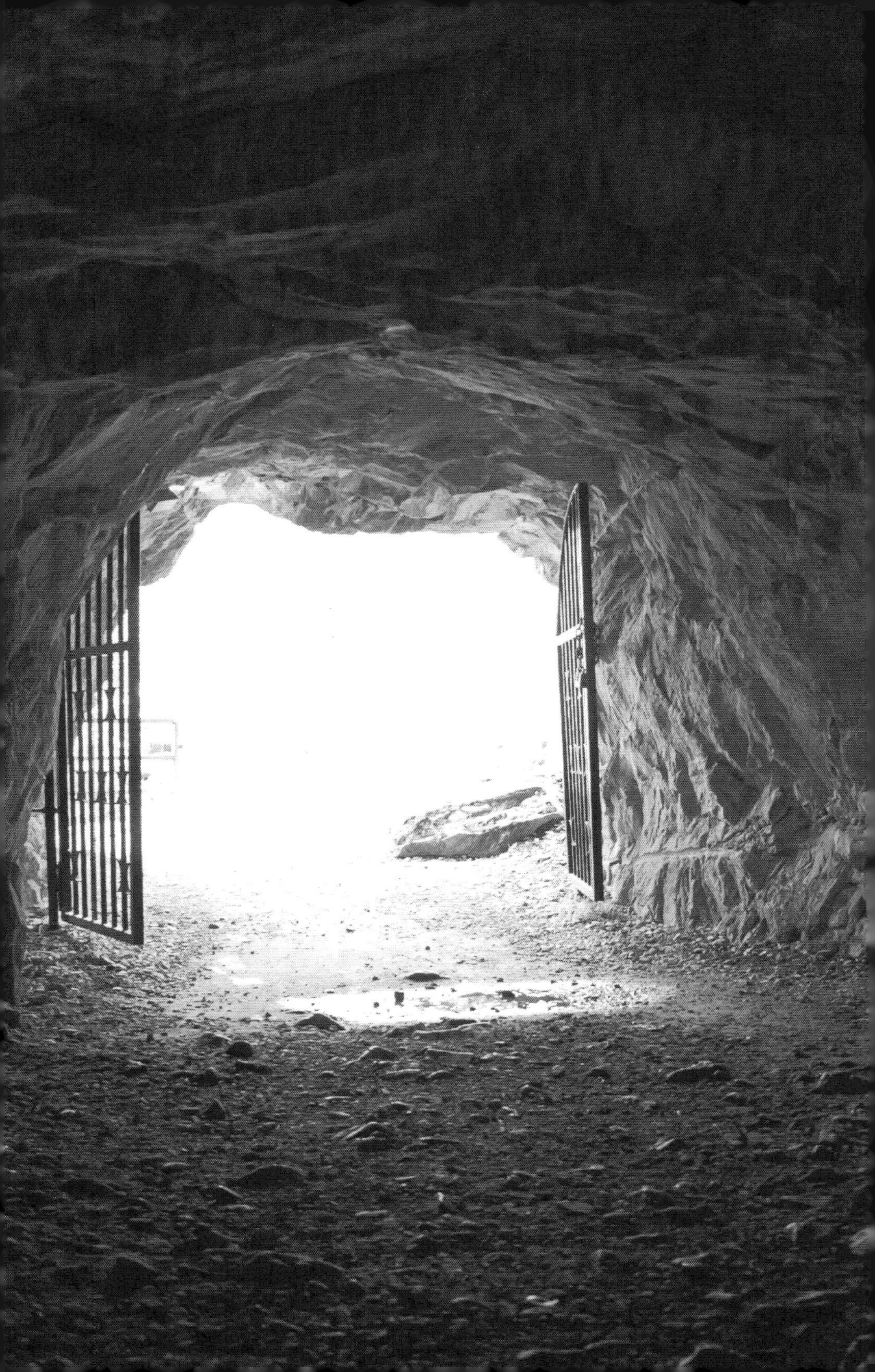

Thursday Febuary 17th
7:48pm

 This is hard. Monday was Valentines Day. He bought me flowers and took me to my doctor's appointment. We kind of connected, but then Wednesday came. He said his mother called and said she was coming into town, so he told me to figure it out because he hasn't told anyone that I wasn't at the house.

 So today he was racing home and it kind of made me mad, because who was he in a hurry to go see. And then I found a red and black string of hair in my seat, but I was like, ok maybe it came off of me. I mean I am in hair school after all. So, I don't know. Right now, I don't know what to do. I'm lost. I'm trying to access you GOD, because I need to speak with YOU!!

Friday Febuary 18th
7:47pm

Papa, I miss him, but I'm afraid that in reality there's really nothing to miss. I'm afraid he's talking to other woman, and I'm over here playing the fool.

Papa, I praise your holy name, please help me to turn my face from darkness and sin the way You turn Yours when I do it or anyone else does it. Help me to not be in the presence of evil, sin, darkness, or wickedness. Take it away from me, take it away from my children and family. Heal and deliver Nicholas from it. Please Father, hear my prayers for my marriage, my husband, myself, my children, my family, and everything that pertains to me here on earth.

Lord, please come and see about us, heal us, deliver us, and restore us.

In JESUS Name Amen.

As the days went by, we got into a routine. He would pick me up early in the morning, and I would ride home with him in the afternoon. He would stay a while to spend time with the kids before they went to bed.

At first, we didn't talk, I knew GOD was telling me to remain silent toward him. After a while it got hard, then just impossible to not talk to him. We would stop for breakfast in the morning on the way to work and school. He would try to create conversation and I would keep it short. Eventually, the enemy knew what to say to get a conversation stirred up in me. I would go on and on and then get out the car feeling guilty for not obeying the LORD's commandments. I was slowly being desensitized, almost forgetting that I was fighting a war for my husband's salvation. I was slowly settling into a mindset that our current situation was ok. I was forgetting about the assignment. I had forgotten that this move was not meant to be comfortable, but just the next step in getting my marriage restored. I was settling for conversation instead on a kingdom unity. The devil was easing his way back into my life and he started with communication. Thats how he always starts.

    The voice of the Lord towered over my emotional needs. CUT HIM OFF!!

My mom soon found out I was at her house, and she asked me what happened. I simply said GOD told me to come here. Of course, like any mother who wants her child to be happy, she questioned my discernment and if I really heard that from GOD and not the enemy. I wasn't alarmed given her perception of my marriage. My husband is a good man, he takes care of his family and now I have broken up a good thing because of what I thought I heard GOD say. Well last time I read, the enemy appeals to the flesh, and I wanted nothing more than to be with my husband. From my experiences nine times out of ten, when my heart is being tugged to do something, I really don't want to do, it's more than likely GOD.

I was being deemed crazy to my family, and I had no case to back me up. Even my sisters asked me if I was sure, I said yes, confidently. God had set me in the midst of a jury ready to throw the scriptures at my logics. Even my husband called and said GOD hates divorce. I couldn't believe it! Out of all the times I talked about the bible, that's the scripture he could understand the most. I was feeling persecution, even by sermons at church. We would attend church on Sundays, and sometimes my husband would take us. Hoping that GOD would release a word to convict my husband about him not surrendering, or the LORD, justifying my leaving. No, Instead, I left offended. Messages that confused me were preached. The pastor spoke about; "If someone walked out of your life, let them go. If they couldn't stand by you in the rough times, then they weren't meant to be. Hearing my husband clear his throat on that one, made my blood boil. I wanted to stand up so many times and say, "What if GOD told you to leave." Why did he never preach about not being unequally yoked. Lord why weren't you defending me.

I was angry with GOD, not only was everyone and everything going against what I had just proclaimed to be a revelation from the LORD, but now I was questioning my decision. I didn't leave voluntarily.

I was commanded by GOD.

The noise of everyone around me, made me question what I knew for sure I heard GOD say. Convicted by sermons on, "Loving thy neighbor," and questions at school on why I never wore my wedding ring. It became a lot, and very overwhelming. Not to mention the overall sadness I was feeling for missing my husband and our life together.

I was starting to look like the one in the wrong. My family was torn, and from the outside looking in I was the one to blame. I prayed to GOD day and night to save my marriage. Some nights it would end in praise and worship filling the room, and the Power of The HOLY SPRIT filling my body, allowing me to understand this must be done. That it was all a part of GOD'S Master Plan. Other nights it would end in me feeling defeated, with tears streaming down my face, in confusion. Not knowing why GOD would allow me to experience this. Even though I was in a house full of people I felt alone, scared, and unsure of what was happening in my life. Yet, no matter how uncertain I was, I knew GOD was in control. Many days I cried and yearned for my life, not realizing I was becoming like the children of Israel in the wilderness. A place where I once felt oppressed, unappreciated, and hindered. A place, where I cried out to GOD to be delivered from, I now was yearning and seeking to return to again. Maybe I "thought" I wanted to be delivered, maybe it wasn't so bad after all. I mean I could handle being with my husband until he got saved. Our marriage wasn't violent, or unfaithful, just unequally yoked.

In mid thought, I heard the HOLY SPIRIT say, "DON'T SETTLE."
Immediately I knew he wanted me to keep going. Keep fighting until I saw the change I had been praying about. I was just unsure if I had the strength to fight. I just felt like I had been fighting for so long already. Was it even working?

Fighting a fight like this takes spiritual courage. The courage to say that even when the odds are stacked against you, and everyone speaks negative about the decisions you have made as a believer; you still acquire the drive to keep pressing toward the mark. I knew in my heart deep down what GOD had asked me to do, but as time went on the opinion of others and my own personal desires, started to sound a lot like GOD'S voice as well. Thoughts like, "Maybe it's times to go back home. Or "Maybe GOD wanted to show me to stop complaining about where He had me planted. These thoughts tormented my mind. Maybe GOD wanted to teach me a lesson. Jesus never condemned anyone for their sin, He only told them the truth. Maybe I was being put in time out for the condemnation towards my husband's sin, and him not following JESUS'S way.

Days turned into weeks and weeks turned in to months. The feeling of GOD being silent about this matter made me antsy. I wanted the confusion to go away. I wanted to be at ease about whatever steps I took moving forward. I read books on loving your husband in the faith and watched videos on how GOD restored marriages that had been broken, and unequally yoked. I prayed hard and wondered when my miracle would come. When my husband would visit the children, I eagerly looked for signs in change in his behavior or speech about GOD, but it all appeared to be the same as when I left.

    Some days I would feel over it, why am I standing in the gap and praying for somebody who doesn't even want you, GOD. He doesn't desire to change or have a relationship with you. The HOLY SPIRIT would come and humble me, and remind me that, that is exactly what JESUS did. He died for me, and the world, even when we didn't want Him either. Even when we were still blind to GOD, and still in our sin. I felt guilty for even thinking that. I had to apologize to GOD. Who did I think I was to complain about praying for someone who was lost, especially if the person was someone I loved. That next Sunday, A sermon was preached. The pastor spoke about it being better to stay and work it out, and to fight together than separate. It was like that was all I needed to hear before I had the okay to go back home. Immediately after church I told my husband the good news. I told him I was coming home. I could tell he was excited but not like I thought he would be. Over this journey I realized I have watched to many fairy tale movies, and way too much lifetime. I pictured him shouting to the church, "My wife is coming home!! Well, it didn't happen that way, but I took what I could get. Impatiently he helped pack my bags at my mother's house to bring his family home. I was homesick and ready to return. The car ride was pleasant. I hadn't seen my husband this happy internally in a long time. To say the least I was excited to. I had missed him so much. When I returned home the house felt cold and dark. It looked the same as the day I left. I had been only gone for about four months, but I at least thought It would be changed up a bit. Not sure why I thought that. My husband was never big on switching things up, I was the decorator. Besides the memorable view, the home felt like it had no life, kind of like an old shack. A home that was once filled with life now felt like no one lived there. It was in that moment that I realized when I left that day, so did the HOLY SPIRIT. The same SPIRIT that hovered over the waters in Genesis when the book said, "And then there was life," had left too. After about a week I felt at home. Dusting, deep cleaning, even some decorating, made me feel welcomed again. My mom, who was happy to have her home back, would call often explaining how she missed the grandchildren being there. My husband started looking better and happier, and I was determined to find as many solutions to fight for our marriage as possible. It was nice to be back at home, it was my comfort place.

CHAPTER 4

THE JOURNEY BACK HOME

The curse of the Lord is in the house
of the wicked: but He blesseth the habitation
of the just.
                                    Proverbs 3:33 KJV

The first week of me being home we sat down and talked for a long time. I told him I wanted to go to church as a family. Occasionally we went, but this time I meant faithfully. I wanted to learn more about how to run our household, as children of GOD. I wanted us to be kingdom parents and raise godly children. I wanted us to learn about finances so that we could lenders and not borrowers. I even wanted us to take the marital classes that they had at the church, so we could learn how to stand against the tricks and schemes of the devil and fight as a kingdom family. Fight for our children and our generations to come. I told him I wanted us to start praying together in the morning and at night. He agreed. He had stopped smoking, and I was so proud of him. He was changing and I was ready to help him.

My husband intentionally started making time for me, which was one of my issues from times in the past. I tried to accommodate with creating dinner dates for us at home, since he was always busy. Things were changing and I was happy. We were sitting in service one morning when the pastor called all the young people under thirty to come down. It seemed like the whole church stood up. At that time, me and my husband were both under thirty, so as we made our way down the aisle with our children this massive crowd followed. The bishop was moved with the amount of young men that were there. As he stretched forth his hand to pray over us, something happened. I felt the Spirit of GOD move in that place. As he prayed for the chains of our generation to be broken off of us, my husband and several others began to weep. As I reached out to grab his shoulder his hand met mines, and I felt his burdens. He was weak and tired. And was trying but didn't know the way. The car ride home he seemed emptied out. Crying before the Lord, has a way of doing that to you. A little after that someone called and needed him to do something that was not convenient for him to do. He immediately got angry. Now knowing my husband who says yes to anything someone ask's him to do whether he wants to do it or not, I was aware that this was an attack from the enemy. The devil was mad, Nick was being set free, and that means he was losing another one. I tried to remain calm but then he turned around and snapped on me. At first, I knew it wasn't him, but then he struck a nerve, so I snapped back. By the end of the day, we had cooled down and apologized to each other. The devil had used us both.

    Determined to see what blessing GOD had for us this coming Sunday, I laid the children's clothes out the night before. The next morning, I woke up I heard the Holy Spirit say (streamline.) So, I guess weren't going to church today. I got back in the bed and streamlined one of me and my husband's favorable preachers. He's young like us so it's easy to relate to his teachings. I woke him up and told him this is how we were going to do church today.

    We watched the sermon together and I took notes. After, the pastor gave an alter call, and my husband who was standing up out the bed raised his hand. In disbelief, I kept praying with me eyes away from him. I didn't want to embarrass him, but I was so proud of him. After the salvation prayer I turned and went to him and gave him a big hug. I kissed him and told him I was proud of him, for giving his life to JESUS.

We were enjoying being back together. It was like I never left. My husband and I have this weird connection where we can be away from each other, or something drastic can happen and we can pick up like it has always been ok. I knew GOD had created us for each other, it was just fighting the good fight to keep it. A few weeks after my husband gave his life to GOD I was lying in bed when I heard a voice say to me, "Feed him psalms 1-3 slowly." I rolled out of bed and asked GOD how. Nick would pray with me sometimes, but reading the scriptures to him was a whole different thing. I had forgotten what GOD had asked me to do, partly because I didn't know how to do it. Usually, when I sent him things pertaining to GOD either he wouldn't mention it, or I would ask him if he watched it, and he would say not yet. So I left it alone.

Things were going good between me and Nick, but I started noticing my drive for JESUS was slowly going down. I wasn't praying as often, and fasting wasn't a thing. I didn't have an interest in reading the Word of GOD. I would lay in the bed and look at the closet and feel GOD tugging and calling me to come, but it was like something was blocking me from coming. The inside of me wanted to come, but my flesh was weak. I was too lazy to get up and go. My prayer life was going down, and I even started to let out a curse word or two. Seeing the changes in my spiritual drive overtook my happiness in my marriage. Not only was I slowly losing a desire to spend time with GOD, but I also discerned that I was slowly dying as well, spiritually. I couldn't here GOD. There was no flame, no spark, it felt like I was being separated from GOD. I couldn't be happy; it wasn't supposed to be this way. I imagined after my marriage was restored my husband and I would both be moving closer to GOD, not away from Him.

After a while the LORD had stopped calling for me, and it began to seem dark. I remembered going to sleep and waking up and seeing something demonic in the bed between me and my husband. Then I knew it was time to pray. I had been so wrapped up in my husband and us being together, I had gotten off track with my faith, and put GOD on hold. I put my relationship with my husband before GOD, and NO ONE goes before GOD! Searching for GOD, I began reading the scriptures but no presence. I missed Him, I missed His presence. GOD'S presence was nowhere to be found. I cried out and prayed earnestly. The scripture came to me "Seek the LORD while He may be found."

Tears flowed down my face knowing I had taken GOD'S call for granted. I had stopped dreaming, I couldn't discern the atmosphere, and biblical understanding was far from me. It was like I had lost my spiritual gifts, and connection with the LORD. Not soon after I noticed my husband was slipping back into his old ways. With my relationship with

GOD on the rocks all I had was my marriage. I tried everything I could to fight this time for it. I tried watching sermons with my husband even social media videos on other Christian couples. At first, he would watch them with me, then he would just fall asleep in the middle of it. Uninterested, he seemed to not want to know about Christ. We even had conversations about JESUS being the only way to this thing called life. I just felt like I was forcing faith on him again. Here we were again, back where we started. I was begging for his time again, and it was getting harder and harder to get him up for church. He would have an attitude for being up that early. Progress in our marriage had come to a halt.

    I was sleeping in bed one night, when I heard the voice of the LORD say, "because you have forsaken me, you will be as a wife forsaken in her youth. I wept bitterly; I knew the LORD was mad with me. I pleaded for mercy, and HIS grace. Somehow, I knew I was about to go through. I knew I was on GOD's bad side. When I went to my bible to read I landed on Isaiah chapter 59 verses 1 and it read,

"Behold, the Lord's hand is not shortened, that it cannot save; neither his ear heavy, that it cannot hear:
"But your iniquities have separated between you and your GOD, and your sins have hid his face from you that He will not hear." KJV

I had forgotten about GOD. I had been like the children of Israel, once GOD had given them the promise, they went into the land and did the things GOD told them not to do, and they forgot about Him.

    I find it strange how so many believers talk about how kind, and merciful GOD is, and never what HE'S like when you disobey him. I now realize it's because some may not really know Him. Many people that knew my mother raved about how she was a sweet, kind, gentle giant of a woman. While all those things were true, those who really knew her, knew she had a side about her that said she didn't play with her kids, and nobody else for that matter. That lady has a side nobody wanted to experience, or be in the vicinity of, if she felt disrespected. This is the same with GOD, especially for those that know Him. Hebrews 12 speaks,

> **" My dear child, don't shrug off GOD'S discipline,**
> **but don't be crushed by it either.**
> **It's the child He loves that he disciplines;**
> **the child he embraces, he also corrects.**

GOD has a Fatherly anger, and a disrespected wrath, and what I was feeling was the disappointment of a Father, the anger of my LORD. I knew I couldn't stand against GOD, I had to sit in this one. I had to understand this was nothing to be taken lightly. I was in trouble, and I needed Him to come. But I had a feeling He was going to let me wait and think about this one.

    I heard him call me on a fast. It was a twenty-four-hour water fast. I didn't know what to expect on this fast, but I was just trying to get to GOD. I was also determined to understand what had happened to me, and to us. I thought we were moving toward restoration and being equally yoked. He began to put me on one fast after another. The more I fasted, I saw the LORD pulling me away from my husband again. This time, Nick recognized it too. I wasn't happy with the way GOD was pulling me away. Nick asked me if he had done something wrong. I told him no, that I just needed some time to be alone. I didn't know what to say. GOD had told me to be silent in this time. I was slowly beginning to hear GOD'S voice again. I cried out to him because I needed Him. I felt blocked off from Him. Like a stranger, and not a daughter. Like this time, He was making the Journey back to Him slow and hard. But I soon found out that wasn't the case. That wasn't the case at all.

    After a three-day water fast, the Lord allowed me to see what really happened. I had fell back asleep. I had stopped praying for my husband. The habits he had stopped were rising again. I had fallen asleep in my faith, and the enemy knew it. He waited until I was so wrapped up into my husband again, that I didn't see him unraveling everything we had worked so hard for. The enemy had come in like a flood and I needed the LORD to lift up a standard. I couldn't see where I was. I felt so lost, the enemy had knocked me back several miles from the Kingdom. I was that one that needed JESUS to come and get her. GOD continued to separate me from Nick, and call me to fast and pray. Despite the loneliness, I recognized, not only was I being restored back to the LORD, but I also had a chance to sit back and really watch my husband. I observed him and saw, he didn't want what I wanted. He wasn't done having fun in the world. He wasn't ready to surrender his sin. But it was weighing both of us down. The pressure of me wanting him to change, was like as an ox wanting to do the work and run the race and plowing with a donkey who's stubborn. This is when GOD dropped and released, one of the greatest revelations and one of my bestselling books. I've Never Seen a Sheep on a Leash. Not only was GOD dealing with me about my relationship with Him. He was also showing me that He loves my husband to. And as long as I was trying to pull him along with me, I would eventually make him not want GOD at all.

The LORD, revealed to me that His people are like sheep, easily gone astray. Yet, GOD doesn't even put them on a leash and force them to come back. If their His people, and He's patient enough to wait, then who are we to put stipulations and leashes on our fellow peers.

Not wanting to throw GOD at him, I tried to find common ground and focus on other areas of our marriage, like finances, and communication. I asked him to start a journal with me to help us gain better communication skills. I thought if we made it intimate or maybe like an activity, it would be fun. He told me he's not big on writing. My husband has never been one to express himself, so communicating was a little challenging at times. I was becoming frustrated with him. Our marriage was slowly drying back up and I was being pulled me away from someone that wasn't willing to do the work. He wasn't ready to go all in. Marriage is more than a house, love and kids. Marriage was our foundation for our family. Marriage is work. I was trying to explain to him that if our foundation isn't strong, when the enemy comes and test our faith, loyalty, and love for each other and GOD, we won't stand. Our marriage will then fall and crumble because it wasn't built upon a rock, that's JESUS. It was like beating a dead horse. I didn't understand why he didn't care, why he wasn't trying to change, at least for me. Did I not matter enough, for him to want better for him and us. Many days I cried, just from the journey alone. I would seek time from my husband, but he would be to busy playing his game all night with his friends. No longer was I willing to be humiliated to bed my husband for time with him, ask him to come to bed so I wouldn't be alone, or try to work on us.

 Why Lord, why did you pick me to walk this one out. This is too much. This is too hard. I'm trying to make sure I can stay out of sin and trouble. It was just too much. From my perspective, I was praying, covering our family, children, and household alone. With no help from the head. Every day I was in a spiritual battle. The devil was swinging at me left and right. I was trying to hang on, but I was angry. I was angry with my husband. He was constantly bringing sin in the camp, and GOD constantly had me fasting and praying for him. I was tired, I felt used, mad, abused.

WHEN LORD, WHEN!!!!!!!!!!!! I exclaimed. Why are we still here. I had so much rage in my heart. I just wanted a normal life again and my husband was walking around like everything was still normal and it wasn't. I felt like he was the one to blame. The reason we weren't restored yet.

Months went by of us not talking and sleeping in the same bed. I kept hearing GOD say not to talk to him, to separate myself from him. It was hard not to talk to him, he was my best friend before I met JESUS. It has always been easy for me and my husband to be around each other. I believe that's why him not being big on communicating, never really made or broke our relationship. We just got each other. We worked well together, and we didn't even have to speak, I just really liked to talk.

While all of this was happening in my life, my husband never knew none of this was going on with me. I knew he wouldn't understand. I knew what I was going through only I could go through it. I knew this journey was meant for me, and this walk, I had to walk alone.

It seemed as though my relationship with GOD was going slower this time, getting back to where we were together felt like I was taking baby steps. I was that one that went astray, and the longer you wonder off and do not return. Is the longer it will take to get back to HIM. All the leg work I had done, it seemed as though I had lost it all.

Like I had been pushed back to the beginning. Like I was drinking milk again instead of eating meat. I once heard this woman of GOD say, stay focused and don't get distracted because if you fall back in sin, you don't know how long it will take you to get back up. My life was starting all over again, we had been separated once before, it was all to familiar. Was I back in the wilderness? Was it not time to come back to Nick? Unsure of why GOD was separating us again. Having to go through this heartbreak again, was breaking me down in a way I really couldn't explain. I was losing hope of GOD even doing what He said He would do. I wondered at times was I being played with. Why does it take all of this LORD, why is it taking this long to get my breakthrough.

After another three-day water fast, many things had been revealed. -I went back before it was time. I went back before I saw the change. I had settled, when the Holy Spirit told me not to. I had made my way back to Egypt. I had put my marriage back together, before GOD said it was time. When I thought about it, I never actually heard GOD tell me to go back, like I heard Him tell me to leave. I was now sitting on my living room floor, and I couldn't believe I was back in bondage. My money had started slowing down again, and confusion clouded my mind. I was a slave again, and now I needed the Lord to rescue me AGAIN.

CHAPTER 5

DESPERATION THE JOURNEY BACK TO GOD

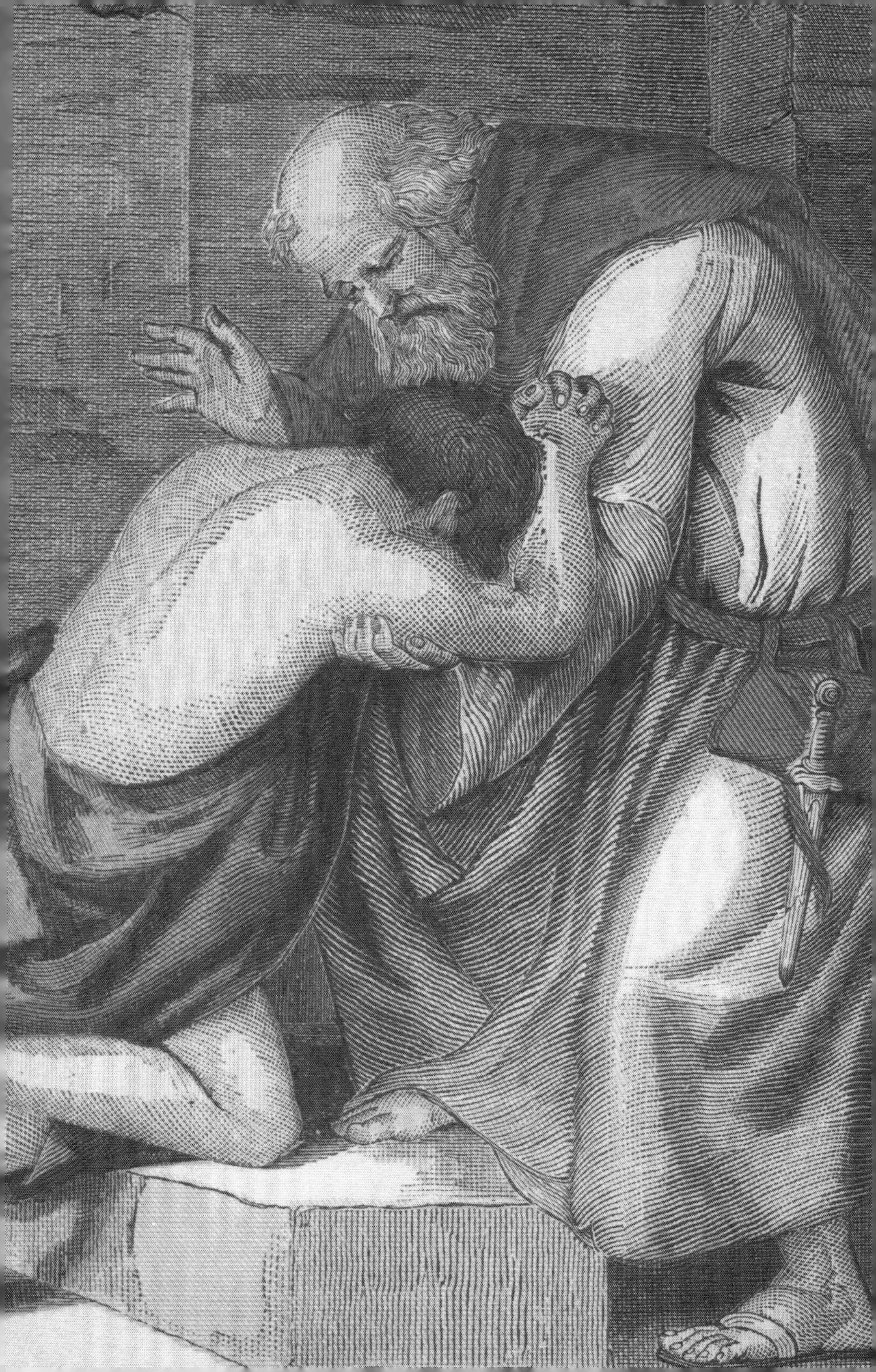

The enemy was fighting me for my life. I had returned to his camp, his trap that was set for me. He lured me back in with my own desires to see my marriage restored. I knew this was going to be a rough fight, but I was determined to be free again. I was miserable my husband started back doing the things that used to make me upset. I started looking at my life and wondered how did I got back here. Why wasn't my marriage restored yet. Why hasn't my husband been delivered. What was GOD waiting on.

LORD, I have been fighting for so long. Why wasn't my husband fully saved yet.

Watching other kingdom marriages and their testimonies on how GOD restored them, allowed bitterness to grow in my heart. But that wasn't the only thing that was festering in the corners of my hardened heart. Watching these couples and realizing how long some of them took to be restored, even after divorce, welcomed disappointment and discouragement as well. Some days I laid in the bed not wanting to do nothing. Laziness and procrastination held me. My hope was dying, and so was my spiritual life. I was in the ring with the enemy, and I was getting knocked out left and right. Barely standing, I felt my strength being ripped away from me like Samson when Delilah cut his hair. Samson had gone back to a relationship that only wanted to drain him. He thought it was time for love, but an enemy was lurking, desiring to strip him of the power that gave him his victory. His relationship with GOD.

That's what the enemy was after, my relationship with GOD

Wrapped and held down by all this demonic oppression I couldn't get up. The bible says that once your delivered and you go back, the demons come back seven times worse, and its even harder to be delivered. Laziness had me paralyzed. I didn't know where I was half the time. Caught back in the cycle of everyday life of just trying to take care of the kids, the household and maybe myself I couldn't keep up with the days. There were times when I didn't even want to do my hair or hygiene I would sit in the closet, upset with GOD. What's happening and why am I not moving. I believe the only thing that kept me on life support were the fast GOD constantly called me to. Furious with the Lord, I questioned why He kept making me fast, when was Nick going to fast. Why was my family enjoying the king's delicacies and I was suffering. I didn't understand. I was like David. The Lord's hand was upon me heavy and who can stand against Him. No One!

I finally got up and went to church. The sermon was powerful enough to feed my feeble spiritual body and get it to take the next step in this journey. He said, DON'T GO BACK!!!!! The word hit me like a spiritual splash of water. I knew he was talking directly to me. He said GOD said, there's nothing back there for you, stop going back. After that God called me to a twenty-one-day water fast. This changed my life forever. One day during the fast I laid face down on the couch dying. Already purposed in my mind i was going to eat, I cried and apologized to GOD. Immediately my eyes closed and I saw my self being carried over a mountain by whom I knew without a shadow of a doubt was JESUS. He had me over his shoulder as he carried my dead like body over what I couldn't finish on my own. I cried even harder. JESUS was willing to keep fighting for me even when I was willing to give up. So I kept going, realizing I was no longer alone, nor doing this in my own strength. What I thought I wouldn't make it through, ended up being what GOD used to get some of those demons off of me. Strength was coming back to me. I could feel it. I had more energy, and my desire for GOD and His Word was rising again. Yes, some days I felt my spirit declining again, but I knew JESUS was right there to bottle feed me. The devil wasn't giving up without a fight. He wasn't letting me go again. He remembered the light I shined last time I had gotten free. I was a threat to the kingdom of darkness. He knew it and I was just being informed. One slave being free, tends to give hope to the rest. Not only was I fighting for my life for freedom with JESUS, but I was fighting for my family's too.

    A fast has a way of opening your eyes to the truth and getting them out of your flesh. The spiritual understanding was all coming back to me. This fight wasn't even about me. It was about the enemy losing souls, and GOD was winning more. What if Harriett Tubman and the other slaves that helped her reach freedom, would have given up because of the affliction coming up against them. Or what if they decided to go back, because they were afraid of what was ahead. Where would African Americans be? Would anyone think it was possible to be free? Of course, GOD, always finds someone else, if not her then someone. When I looked at it this way, I was determined that I wanted GOD to use me to set the captives free. Use me GOD to break generational curses in my family. Please don't find anybody else LORD, please use me. I had understood that if I didn't fight this fight, this would be a battle that would fall on my children. And I didn't come this far with GOD, to let the mantle be dropped here. I was ashamed of where I found myself, back in the same vomit GOD had already delivered me out of. I felt JESUS'S hand reaching out to help me up again, and it was time for me to be done dwelling in my sorrows. It was time for me to stand up and fight. And fight the only way that would win, with the WORD. I started taking my time with JESUS more seriously. I stopped focusing so much on what the enemy was doing, and started watching for what GOD was getting ready to do. Excited to see my desire for GOD coming back in my life, my health sprung forth as well. The LORD was with me again. My strength was here, ready to pour into me and I was ready to receive. I needed HIM, like I had never needed anyone else before. I loved JESUS, and I finally realized I had left HIM behind for a man, that didn't even have time for me. Honestly, being bound in sin, you're barely making it to have time for yourself. I couldn't blame him anymore for where our marriage stood. It was in GOD'S hands, not ours. It was time for me to get back on my feet, and then and only then would I be useful for the Kingdom of GOD.

CHAPTER 6

MOVE FORWARD

It's been a whole year since I realized what went wrong. Since I understood where I had been. And Now I'm fighting back. Lord this has been the rockiest, toughest, most exhausting year of my life. Yet in this year alone I have watched You bring rivers in the desert. I watched You move mountains into the sea and slay giants right in front of me. You exposed my enemies and removed them too. LORD, you have done great and mighty things for me in this year alone. But it was hard. I filed for a divorce, like you told me to. I started really cutting all ties with Nic.

We said nothing to each other, he would get angry and ask me why I was being disrespectful. I really wasn't trying to; I was obeying GOD. Every time we would start talking back, I would hear GOD say cut him off. And so I would have to all over again stop talking to him. This process went on for a while. Why was it so hard to cut him off. My heart would hurt from not talking to him. It even got to the point to where I was hearing him talk about me to himself after a situation occurred between us. I didn't know how to cut him off. I struggled with this for a while, and when I say a while, really the whole year. It looked as if I was trying to be cruel and mean to him, but I wasn't. I had to get to the point where I wasn't going to worry about what he thought about me, and just obey my Heavenly Father.

I believe for the most part I was confused as to why a GOD that tells us to love thy neighbor would have me treat my husband so bad. It wasn't until I actually started obeying consistently, that I saw why I was commanded this order from the LORD. Silence is key in situations like this. From my point of view, with me finally being taught on how to hold my tongue, GOD was revealing every body's heart to me. My husbands, family members and friend's. If you listen, people will actually tell what's in their hearts about you. To my surprise, GOD wasn't only showing me other hearts but mine as well. I saw anger in my heart towards others that had offended me, unforgiveness, and bitterness towards others and my husband. The command of silence was GOD'S way of keeping me from incriminating myself and hurting others with my words. It is true what they say, hurt people, hurt people.

There were several occasions where I felt my husband did something inconsiderate or disrespectful and I had a whole dialogue typed in my head on how I was going to serve him my defense. Unfortunately, because it wasn't GOD'S will for me to be speaking to him, my obedience kept me in a light that only the LORD Himself could have shined on me. I was hurting, and I needed him to know. At first I was angry at GOD, He watched people call and disrespect me for the way I was treating my husband. He watched, my husband talk to me like I hadn't tried to save our marriage and fight for it before we got to this point. And other things between these moments that left me looking weak and defenseless. I didn't understand, but I was determined to get to the bottom of it. A couple months went by of my bitter silence strike and my husband had called to tell me his mom was coming over, but she was down the street.

Now most wives know when guest come over you like to clean your house and prepare you mind for company. I suppose he had started this trend of telling me things moments before it would happen or just not at all, to punish me for not talking to him. Whatever the reason, I had had it. I was fed up. I immediately called him back and gave him a piece of my hurting, bitter heart. He was silent as I chewed him out about my time being valuable just as his was. After I hung up the phone surprisingly, I felt great. I was finally able to plead my case, stamp, and seal it. There were no guilty christian convictions in my heart, well at least not right away. After about ten minutes I felt the conviction of the Holy Spirit pulling at my heart to go and pray. I came to the closet, like a child being called in to be disciplined by her father. I hung my head low as I opened my bible wondering what verse GOD would give me now.

Mathew 6:14
"For if ye forgive men their trespasses, your heavenly Father will also forgive you." KJV

I didn't even cry, which is usually the response I have when I get in trouble by GOD, but nope, no tears. I was too angry to cry. I was done being humiliated, disrespected, and mistreated. I was finally sticking up for myself, and I get in trouble. But nevertheless, not my will LORD, your will be done. So, I called him back and apologized, because in all reality I represent GOD, not me. So I must come correct. when I hung up the phone, I was sorrowful to JESUS how I acted. He showed myself taking a shovel and digging up that old me, who had been laid to rest. Through my silence JESUS was building up a resistance in me to fight back with my words. Something that been a stronghold all my life. He was teaching me I was no longer apart of the world, and here in the kingdom that wasn't how they did things. I was disgusted with my behavior and the fact that I let someone else take me back to something I was being delivered form.

    This year hasn't been only hard, but beautiful. The LORD blessed me with my own business and remodeled my whole salon. He also blessed me with my very own car, my very first car. There's been so many beautiful gestures, and blessings from my Father this year. It's just been rough. How can your best year be your worst year. Well, I'm sure the children of Israel can relate. The year they finally saw freedom, was the year they had to experience what it was like in the wilderness. They were so angry with their current situation, that they asked Moses did GOD free them just to bring them into the wilderness to die. Wow, what an insult to GOD. Well, that's what I was doing. Insulting GOD, first of all my sin led me here, and to blame GOD for what I was going though was a bit too far. Yes, He allows certain things to happen to us, but to only allow it to teach, shape and mold us into better individuals, for His purpose and glory.

I believe GOD'S will, will be done regardless. Understanding this brings me to the conclusion that because His will, will be done no matter what, the choices and paths we take determine how challenging the journey will be. It would be symbolic to a twenty-four-hour day given to you, by GOD. In that twenty-four-hour journey it is GOD's will for you to see the next day. It's coming whether you like it or not. He has blessed you with it, so it is coming. Now if you have a project due by the next day and you delay and fail to plan properly. If laziness and procrastination have you by the foot. Then these twenty four hours will be the most stressful, nerve racking twenty four hours in your week. But if you wake up early, seek GOD, and get His plan for your day. Even when the enemy throws his distractions your way, you'll still have room to get back on track with the detours GOD will allow you to take.

This Is life. GOD wanted to bless me with all the things He gave me this year. It was His will to do so, but it was hard to get them. Why? Maybe it was a lot harder than usual because I was in a place GOD called me out of. He called me out from amongst unbelievers, and I went back. Sometimes it's harder to receive your blessings because your not where your supposed to be. Or maybe your around people that GOD has called you away from. People that will hinder your success and block your blessings, if you let them. There will be times in life where the LORD will separate you from people because they can't come with you in this next season of your life. But when we override the Lord's command, and go back and get them, you also bring the hell GOD was trying to separate you from with them too. Now your experiencing setbacks and delays and you don't know why. I asked the LORD why it was taking so long for Him to deliver me from this place. Why was I going through all of this. Why was His hand so heavy upon me. He replied. "So you won't go back!"

Paused in disbelief, I rehearsed His words in my head, realizing what He was actually saying. He allowed me to be persecuted and mocked. He allowed me to walk down a path of desperation for so long, that all the desires of wanting this marriage would be out of me. So that when it was all said and done, I wouldn't want to go back. I felt like the children of Israel, who GOD took through the wilderness the long way, so they wouldn't be able to find their way back.

I was now understanding the purpose of everything I thought GOD had forsaken me in. He purposed it to produce purpose and to force me to grow out of the place He was trying to uproot me from, in the first place. My mind was changing like the first time. I didn't care what happened to my marriage. It was GOD'S business no longer mine. I was ready to live and take care of me. I was ready to do GOD'S will right this time.

God told me it was time to go again. Unsure of where he wanted me to go, I inquired of His direction in prayer. This time it was different. I wanted to hear what He had to say. I felt like I had been dragged this whole year, I was tired and ready to be set free. I didn't even recognize myself, I had nothing left to give my marriage or anyone else. GOD was offering me an exit ticket and this time I wasn't going to fumble this one. I was stepping back up to the plate to bat and with the Good LORD on my side I didn't plan on missing this hit. Apart of me was afraid to step out there again. Where was I going to go. What was I going to do without a steady income. He had stopped the flow of clients in my salon, and I was full time working on me. I knew He didn't want me to worry about those things. The Holy Spirit would repeat every now and then, when I got weary, I got it covered. Every time thoughts of what if would creep in my mind He would whisper, He had it covered. And I just had to trust Him.

Remembering the dream I had about Nick and I in the cave, I understood GOD, was calling me higher with Him, and I was waiting on someone who wasn't willing to go. It crushed me so bad. Deep pains moved through my body and soul. Having to walk alone. Having to experience success and miracles without my husband because he wasn't ready to surrender to GOD. For so long I was angry with him, just get up. Just come out of the darkness. Call on Him, speak His name, and He will set you free. I didn't understand. Didn't my husband see my transformation. Why is he hurting me like this. For so long I waited and waited. For so long tears fell from my eyes. For so long I was scared, confused, alone, sad, angry and hurt. Bitterness bound me, anger held me, sorrow kissed me, but

GOD. JESUS held my hand through it all. He needed me to rise up out of that pain so I could see the truth. He needed me to make this journey. If I really loved Nick, I would make this journey for the both of us, so that our generations would have a way paved for them. He was going to use us, **both** of us. He just chose to start with me first. For whom the **SON** sets free is free indeed. Nick was waiting on GOD'S appointed time. He couldn't leave the cave if he wanted too. When you're in sin the enemy has you bound by chains only GOD can set you free, and I prayed that when He finally came for Nick, that my husband would wave the white flag, surrender, and follow JESUS. My prayer was now, Lord, when my previous life is being destroyed help me not to look back, ever again in JESUS name Amen.

    I knew GOD, was going to do something big for us, but it wasn't back there. JESUS kept telling me it was time to move on from that place. There was nothing left there for me.

A LOVE LETTER TO GOD

Here I am ready to take my next step
Afraid, unsure and a little fearful
I leap into your arms, and I dive head first
Lord catch me
and please don't let me fall
Your Word says that I will not be ashamed.
I want to see freedom
freedom and what's on the other side of this battle

Lord walk with me, and hold my hand
And lead me on
Lead me on, me and my three girls to the
Lead me on to the
PROMISED LAND

This book is dedicated to every marriage, that has been asked for by the enemy. I pray that your FAITH, will not fail.

Signed,
Kendryana Scharschmidt.

Made in the USA
Columbia, SC
20 May 2024

a68dd4af-55f6-42c5-a6d5-d27e1edb8427R03